The Next 10 Amendments

In Order To Form A More Perfect Union

Dan Farfan

DAN FARFAN

2nd Edition Copyright © 2010–2013 Dan Farfan

ISBN:1484958306
ISBN-13:978-1484958308

DEDICATION

George Read	DE	Lawyer
Gunning Bedford, Jr.	DE	Lawyer
John Dickinson	DE	Lawyer
Richard Bassett	DE	Lawyer
Jacob Broom	DE	Farmer, Politician
James McHenry	MD	Surgeon
Daniel of St. Thomas Jenifer	MD	Justice of the Peace
Daniel Carroll	MD	Planter
John Blair, Jr.	VA	Jurist
James Madison, Jr.	VA	Statesman, Author
William Blount	NC	Land Owner
Richard Dobbs Spaight	NC	Statesman
Hugh Williamson	NC	Physician, Scholar
John Rutledge	SC	Judge
Charles Cotesworth Pinckney	SC	Lawyer, Scientist
Charles Pinckney	SC	Planter, Statesman
Pierce Butler	SC	Planter, Statesman
William Few	GA	Planter, Statesman
Abraham Baldwin	GA	Minister, Educator
John Langdon	NH	Farmer, Politician
Nicholas Gilman	NH	Military

Nathaniel Gorham	MA	Merchant, Land Owner
Rufus King	MA	Lawyer
William Samuel Johnson	CT	Lawyer
Roger Sherman	CT	Lawyer (self taught)
Alexander Hamilton	NY	Lawyer, Statesman
William Livingston	NJ	Lawyer, Statesman
David Brearley	NJ	Judge
William Paterson	NJ	Judge
Jonathan Dayton	NJ	Military, Lawyer
Benjamin Franklin	PA	Scientist, Author
Thomas Mifflin	PA	Merchant
Robert Morris	PA	Judge, Statesman
George Clymer	PA	Statesman
Thomas FitzSimons	PA	Merchant
Jared Ingersoll	PA	Lawyer
James Wilson	PA	Judge, Statesman
Gouverneur Morris	PA	Statesman, Author
William Jackson	–	Military, Secretary

Proud not just to live in the country they wrought, but also to stand on their shoulders to see over the horizon.

CONTENTS

PREFACE

I'm not a historian, lawyer or a fortune teller, however, I predict that someone you trust recommended this book. No one went to the Internet today to see if the long wait was over for Dan Farfan's follow up to 1995's non-record breaking <u>Life's Great Questions - A Recipe for Mastery</u>. I appreciate the trust you have already demonstrated because it's my trust that brought this book to life. I trust the Declaration of Independence, the United States Constitution, our Founders who risked everything in order to form a more perfect union and the men and women who have served the United States of America bravely in the military and as first responders. Each of them stood on the shoulders of the great men and women who preceded them and for that I'm grateful. It's with great humility I look from their shoulders to offer you my vision, in order to form a more perfect union.

There has only been one other time in history that warranted ten amendments to the U.S. Constitution. Part of the genius of the Bill of Rights is that each amendment stands alone as an important principle and they all fit together to define what we hold dear and who we aspire to be. However, I believe we live in an age that has lost Constitution.

We allow our politicians to swear an oath to preserve, protect and defend it, then demand no consequences when they publicly dismiss it. I wrote this book to be the jolt that wakes us up and sparks discussion and debate, "Who are we today and who do we want to be tomorrow?"

In closing, I have two requests. When you read each amendment consider both the solution offered and the problem identified. You won't agree with everything you read. That's natural. Even the Bill of Rights had (and has) opponents. That's healthy. And when you consider referring the book to someone who trusts you, ask yourself this question, "Should people talk about Constitution?"

Dan Farfan

INTRODUCTION

The dictionary definition of the word constitution I find most interesting contains two words, fundamental and principles. It is one thing to declare independence, even articles of incorporation do that for a company. But codifying in writing the fundamental principles on which an organization operates is a step rarely taken.

Sure, companies hire consultants to draft a mission statement and lists of visions and values that get plastered on employee ID badges, but a corporate constitution is almost never found. Instead companies have policies and procedures, so they have legal standing to fire people who break the rules. But where is the corporate Bill of Rights? And equally important, what is the amendment process?

Fortunately, Founders of the United States understood from history and personal experience that such a loose commitment between the governed and the governing would never create a just country with free citizens. A contract is needed (ironically for the same reasons businesses have contracts with each other) so that everyone knows where they stand, what they can expect and what's expected from them, which is precisely the function of a constitution. Thank goodness for the United States Constitution.

But a not so funny thing has happened on the way to our third century birthday, we lost Constitution. Ask strangers on the street to identify three U.S. Supreme Court Justices, the last amendment ratified, or to name any issue due before the court in the near future and they will likely give you blank stares. While it is simple to throw stones at the education system or "the media" or even the population itself, I believe the main culprit behind citizens' loss of Constitution is success.

Despite flaws, speed bumps and maddening inefficiencies, United States of America just works. Ask an immigrant from a country that doesn't work. They'll tell you. America works. Constitution works. Most people can't answer a simple question about the internal combustion engine either. But they get in a car, turn the key, gas it up from time to time and if new oil happens twice a year, jackpot. To most of us the country works with even less care than an automobile, so of course almost no one really understands the internal workings. The most common witticism American politicians throw to defend the dirty secrets of legislating is, "There are two things you never want to see made, sausage and laws." Oh really?

Who do you suppose that "pay no attention to the (mostly) men behind the curtain" policy benefits? It's always the people behind the curtain. The phrase I chose to guide my exploration of Constitution is from the financial world, "past performance is not an indicator of future results." If the financial meltdown of 2008 and the Great Recession that followed taught us anything, it should be that relying on what you've always relied on is not just the absence of strategy, but it's just plain foolish.

I believe for the country to continue to just work no less than a revival of Constitution is required. And what better way to revive Constitution in the hearts and minds of Americans than to sharpen our computers (I don't own a pencil or a quill) and debate ten new amendments? While the country does just work, room for improvement abounds.

Being a Computer Scientist, my amendments arise from a unique approach and reveal a non-traditional perspective than most would expect to see from a historian or a lawyer. Which begs the question, why don't historians and lawyers propose constitutional amendments? Perhaps they think it's perfect, or too old-fashioned to bother. Perhaps they think it would be a waste of time. Perhaps they think themselves to small and it too grand. Perhaps they don't stand to benefit from awakening Constitution. Perhaps the evidence supporting my assertion that we have lost Constitution just got a great deal more compelling.

Unfettered by such concerns, my background allows me too look at the United States of America as a giant, but finite, system of complex systems. My respect for the subject matter allows me to accept Constitution as the proper place where systemic fixes belong. My analysis techniques, a particularly geeky subject for another time, fortunately do not muddle the results offered in the following pages. I provide with each amendment a simple rationale that places the solution in the context of familiar problems and often not so familiar principles.

If you find yourself agreeing with the rationale but not the amendment, then by all means change mine or draft your own solution! Dissent, discussion and debate are the water, oxygen and food of any healthy organization, be it country, government, company or family.

If you find yourself agreeing with an amendment but your initial reaction is, "that will never happen," remember this, the people of the future will make decisions using their current conditions, not ours. If the people in the our Founders' past had not pondered what they had, solved on paper what was broken and finally written what they wrote, then history would've been robbed of the United States of America. Even if it takes decades or centuries to reach implementation, an idea's quality matters, not its age.

According to www.usconstitution.net, the 27th Amendment which changed congressional pay rules was proposed in 1789, but was ratified 1992 (74,003 days later). Our Founders would be proud!

With that bit of trivia under our belt, let us begin our journey of 74,002 days or fewer. I give you <u>The Next 10 Amendments: In Order To Form A More Perfect Union</u>.

AMENDMENT XXVIII

PRESIDENTIAL TERM OF OFFICE

Section 1.

A President is limited to a single ten year term as of the term beginning January 20th, 2021.

Rationale

It's difficult to find anything in modern politics more pathetic or loathsome than the leader of a country who publicly panders to keep a job he already has instead of doing it to the best of his ability in the first place. The ambition to be reelected and fear of the stigma of being a one term failure must no longer cloud judgment, derail decision making, curtail leadership or impede courage.

A decade is an emotional and psychological unit of history. When it belongs to a single President, it will add additional focus beyond that provided by a periodic election timetable. When people with any political sense of history think of the USA in the 80's they think of Reagan. The 90's were Clinton's. The 2000's, George W. Bush. These men won twice and their two terms spanned most of "their" decade, but these two conditions were complete happenstance. The Presidential Term of Office Amendment takes that uncertainty out of the equation. One term, ten years.

The reflexive reaction to this is usually, "too long" primarily because Americans are conditioned to the four year election cycle. It's all they've ever known. Compare ten years to leadership reigns of other industrialized nations over the last 100 years. Ten years is not too long, especially when compared to the freedom to govern not having to win again brings.

Section 2.

Anyone who is an employee, intern, volunteer or contractor in for or to the Executive Branch shall be prohibited from directly or indirectly participating in political party politics in any way other than voting in public elections for a period ending one year following their involvement with the Executive Branch.

Rationale

The separation of campaigning and governing will bring the kind of focus on governing the country deserves from the Executive Branch. Everyone inside the D.C. bubble knows that politics always comes before governing. Most people outside the bubble have been conditioned to believe that the President being the leader of the party is "just how it works" without having any idea how harmful it really is to the country.

This section not only prevents the all too common practice of the sitting President and Vice President campaigning for anyone, but also it prevents contact between any member of the Executive Branch and political party members or proxies.

We elect someone to be President of us all. No longer will leveraging that job to further the ambitions of a political party be constitutional.

Unfortunately the ten year term is not enough to bring governing into the 21st century.

AMENDMENT XXIX

REPRESENTATION

Section 1.

To reduce the inequities, inefficiencies and corruption of political campaigns and the legislative process, effective January 1st 2021, only citizens belonging to one of two parties, the Democrat or Republican, shall be eligible to hold any elected office in the U.S. Federal government. Representation shall operate as amended in section 2 through 9.

Rationale

The two party system has been entrenched by both parties with an insurmountable labyrinth of legislation, regulations, policies and traditions. This unnatural struggle to prevent a third party from emerging ends only when the importance of the parties drastically shrinks. Everyone wins when energy and resources focus on solving actual problems of the citizenry, not manufactured ones of the political process, politicians and pundits.

The Representation Amendment brings a voice for all citizens to the legislative branch of Federal government.

Section 2.

Each of the two parties party shall be allocated

one seat in the U.S. House of Representatives per State district and one seat in the U.S. Senate per State.

Rationale

When majority rule no longer rewards the lust for power, politicians must compete with the best ideas to solve problems. With a 50–50 split, no party can get anything done alone. With the perpetual irrational battle for majority rule removed from the calculus of governing, the rational battle for majority solutions rightly motivates those in whom the sacred right to govern has been conferred by the governed. While at first glance this seems a recipe for perpetual gridlock, the following two Amendments prevent that.

The two pillars which make the sacred duty of political representation viable are the specific privilege of voting and the general mandate to fight the good fight. Today, a lone citizen Democrat in a majority Republican district has no representation in the U.S. House of Representatives because no one representing her would vote her choice or fight her fight. Similarly, in a heavily Republican state, minority Democrats have zero chance of representation in the U.S. Senate. No longer shall the cornerstone of our venerable representative republic be hostage to the happenstance of geography or the serendipity of neighborhood.

Geography robbing a citizen of representation makes no more sense than if zip code curtailed the right of free speech, due process, equal protection, or any other inalienable basic human right, hence the term inalienable – unable to be taken away.

Districts will be redrawn before November 2020 by independent organizations on advice from State legislatures to reduce the number of districts by half to bring sanity to representation. Unjust power grabs by an ever-changing majority in state legislatures no longer change party representation counts in Washington D.C. Once redistricted, a State may not redistrict for the purposes of Federal representation ever again.

Section 3.
Candidates for public office shall compete in elections only against others in their own party and only for seats allocated to their party.

Rationale
Demonizing the "other guys" is wasteful and belittling in every way to everybody. Competing for the privilege to represent people of like mind is an unequaled honor that should be the primary focus of a political campaign.

When Democrat candidates make their best case to Democrat voters that they are the best Democrat for district and country and Republicans do likewise, you know what happens? Democrats become better Democrats and Republicans become better Republicans.

Shifting the direct battle of philosophy away from campaigning and solely to the heart of governing, where it belongs, makes all political leaders better stewards of the office.

Section 4.

Party members shall be allowed to vote in Federal elections only for one person from their party and have no vote regarding the other party's seat. Non-party members shall be allowed to vote in Federal elections for each party's seat. No person shall be a member of a party if they are not eligible to vote in Federal elections.

Rationale

Political parties diminish the potential and performance of politicians to govern. With party power curtailed, citizen power increases.

Section 5.

Party members who voted in the November election shall elect on the first Tuesday of December a Speaker from their party's list of elected office holders for the coming session. Each party shall have a different Speaker for each chamber of Congress.

Rationale

Accountability to citizens forces Speakers to work first for citizens, not for parties or politicians.

The removal of inequities of majority rule removes the need for "majority leader" and "minority leader" elected by those who have been elected. Instead "Republican Speaker of the House," "Democrat Speaker of the House," "Republican Speaker of the Senate," and "Democrat Speaker of the Senate" lead their parties in their respective chamber. This of course forces a few minor changes elsewhere to adjust for the new titles.

Section 6.

Control of the schedule of the U.S. House of Representative and U.S. Senate shall alternate each month between each of the two parties. The U.S. President on January 1st each year shall select a single party to control January's floor schedule for both chambers of Congress.

Rationale
No one group controls either chambers' floor schedule. The best ideas can only win when all ideas get a hearing. No longer shall majority rule violate representation's voting pillar.

Section 7.

Each committee of both chambers of Congress shall be co-chaired by a person elected from/by each party. Committee schedule control shall fall to the party not in control of the Congressional floor schedule.

Rationale
No longer will majority rule unnaturally inhibit representation's fight the good fight pillar.

The output of the Republican controlled committees in January feeds the Republican controlled floor schedule in February. Likewise, the output of the Democrat controlled committees in February feeds the Democrat controlled floor schedule in March, and so on throughout the two year congressional session.

Section 8.

Citizens shall elect only eligible residents of the jurisdiction in question from the appropriate party membership role to represent them. Votes cast for people ineligible, deceased or otherwise unable or unwilling to fulfill the duties of the office on the first day of the term, shall be invalidated. In all cases election victory shall be awarded to the party member who received the most valid votes who is eligible, alive, able and willing to fulfill the duties of office. If an election produces no individual who meets these criteria, another election shall be held until citizens elect a victor.

Rationale
Dead people can't win. Dead people can't represent. Dead people can't serve. Everyone's heart goes out to the spouse and family, but sympathy is an even worse criterion than DNA for choosing which people govern. Democratic elections threw off the chains of rule by divine right centuries ago. This next logical step is much easier than that and long overdue.

Section 9.

A citizen may belong to only one party at a time

for a period of no less than 5 years or belong to no party at all for a period of no less than 5 years.

Rationale
Party membership is allowed, but flipping and flopping to game the election system is not.

Section 10.
A party member elected to represent citizens, or who is appointed by someone who was, shall not switch parties during their term of office.

Rationale
Party membership is allowed, but flipping and flopping to game the system of governing is not.

Section 11.
Only citizens of the United States eligible to vote in Federal elections may contribute, loan or barter money, goods or services to political campaigns, political parties or any organization with even a partially visible political purpose.

Political contributions shall not be limited in size, laundered through third parties or used for any purpose other than political purposes.

Political contribution records shall identify the citizen giver, the receiver, the amount given and the date and time given, shall be published online and shall be freely visible to all within six hours of transfer to the receiver.

Rationale

Citizens can vote. Citizens can contribute. Companies, clubs, organizations, parties, unions or any other formal or informal collection of people or things, and foreigners can't vote or contribute.

Section 12.

Any act committed by a citizen or non-citizen to the contrary of the letter or spirit of this Amendment shall be identified as and punished as Treason.

Rationale

The penalties of Treason make the stakes higher for those who would harm the republic by harming government than the rewards. Yes, citizens may now take the integrity of their government and by extension their country this seriously.

Those who have previously made a purely partisan living have two rational career choices. They can turn their energies to solutions that solve legitimate problems for the betterment of the country (a.k.a. governing) or they can find another line of work.

No more fooling around.

AMENDMENT XXX

LAW MAKING

Section 1.
Specialized law making software that establishes accountability, ensures transparency, fosters creativity and supports the need for the legislative process to advance both pillars of representation, voting and fighting the good fight, shall be used by Congress for all legislation and internal rule making.

Rationale
Legislating is a special function worthy of custom software more sophisticated and tuned to the challenges at hand than a one size fits all "word processor" that doesn't know a bill from a recipe for grandma Jean's triple fudge brownies.

Section 2.
Each section of a bill shall address only a single topic and may not exceed three pages of (10 pt font) plain text. Each section shall exist in legislative language and plain text form, that must align. The click or press of a button on a computing device readily toggles between both.

Rationale
Today, Congress (and others) draft bills in a single form, known as legislative language. This unreadable, tortuous, seemingly tragically

flawed format makes not just the new law, but unmakes previous laws section by section, line by line, and/or word by word at the same time! This format, while ultimately necessary, robs laymen citizens from their right to oversee their legislator's work in progress.

Plain text form represents the exact content of the new law in non-legal language without the rigor of targeting exactly the location of every change to existing law. Plain text communicates to the entire citizenry, not just lawyers, lobbyists and other insiders.

A bill only in legislative language provides adequate cover for any legislator to not "read the bill." Plain text ends that abdication.

The size limitation applies to the plain text form of the law, not the legislative language.

Section 3.

Per Section Voting: Each person eligible to vote on a bill must vote on each section to have their votes considered valid.

Rationale

Per section voting brings even more focus and importance to representation's voting pillar. An old-fashioned single vote on a 2,300 page bill meant something. Specific votes from each legislator on each section means much more.

No longer will rewriting history about this or that part of a bill clutter the political landscape.

Votes will document specific positions and become public record.

Section 4.

Each person eligible to vote on a bill may submit complete alternative language to any section, which people eligible to vote must also vote for or against. The version that receives the most yea votes becomes the operative section in the final bill.

Rationale

No longer will "what we wanted" stories that invoke selective memory fueled abstractions clutter the political landscape. Everyone's best ideas get documented, compete for votes and become public record. Alternatives will no longer be abstract, hallucinations or vapor. They will be public record.

Section 5.

Alternative language for a section may contradict the language of the original section, but not language in other sections.

Rationale

Each section addresses a single topic only, therefore so must each submitted set of alternate language.

Section 6.

Each version of each section shall identify the name of a single member of Congress responsible for the section and it shall be visible to all citizens in realtime during the legislative process, beginning to end.

Rationale
Language magically appearing anonymously from back room committees without attribution is officially no longer worthy of a great nation that values the sacred contract between the governed and the governing.

AMENDMENT XXXI

LEGISLATIVE BENCHMARKS

Section 1.

Because a law is a promise from the governing, not just a demand on the governed, each new piece of legislation shall contain the following additional elements enumerated in Section 2.

Rationale

The governed hire the governing and empower them with the authority to make rules that benefit the governed. Each law must document and demonstrate over time the value it delivers to the governed in order to be worthy of the authority the governed entrusted to the governing.

Imagine if every company had a Corporate Constitution with the level of clarity and accountability found in this Amendment. Not only would investing in that company be a different matter altogether, but also working for that company would be nothing short of liberating, compared to today's norm.

Section 2.
Section 2.1.
Problem statement, per section

Rationale
Accurately, comprehensively and insightfully defining the problem allows the governed an initial glimpse to evaluate the care and respect with which the governing wield the authority to govern entrusted to them.

Section 2.2.
Current benchmark values and details about specific independent and reproducible collection methods used

Rationale
Measuring something today does no good if that same thing can't be measured again later in the same way.

Section 2.3.
Future benchmark values and dates to clearly define threshold measurements of success

Rationale
Detailing future benchmarks achieves a level of accountability from the governing to the governed that has never existed before, but is fully deserved.

Section 2.4.
A date no more than four years in the future that

compels Congress to conduct or sponsor a mandatory review to consider to continue, amend or repeal the law

Section 2.5.
Predictions made by proponents of the bill (future benchmarks)

Section 2.6.
Arguments made during all public debates of the bill by elected and appointed officials and the surrogates, to clarify for future generations original intent

Section 3.
A law that doesn't produce the promised results represented as future benchmarks shall expire automatically on the date specified.

Rationale
Failure is no longer tolerated as anything but a trigger for a better solution.

Section 4.
A law shall contain a roadmap by which its own lifetime ends.

Rationale
A law is successful not when it's used often to punish or even no longer used at all. A law is successful when it's no longer needed to shape decision making and behavior.

AMENDMENT XXXII

CONSTITUTIONAL CHALLENGE

Section 1.
The Governors of the several States shall have the authority to compel the Supreme Court of the United States to rule directly on the constitutionality of any issue according to the details and process specified in this Amendment.

Rationale
The traditional method for laws to be deemed unconstitutional takes too long and allows too much damage to States and citizens before cases work their way to the Supreme Court of the United States. The traditional requirements for legal standing and harm and a majority vote to even hear a case, while still important for traditional Constitutional cases, have no bearing on this new brand of Governor-initiated Constitutional Challenges.

Section 2.
Any duly elected sitting State Governor can call for a vote at any time on any issue described in specific language posed as a yes/no question. This compels every other active or acting State Governor to vote "yes" or "no" within 72 hours to determine by simple majority if the Supreme Court must provide a constitutional ruling.

Rationale
For example, "Does Federal government have the authority under Constitution to compel citizens to purchase a product or service under threat of penalty or sanction? Yes or No."

It should not be simple to legislate near the boundaries of the Constitution. Both sides of the debate must be ready to stand up, make their case and fight the good fight.

Section 3.
The Supreme Court shall hold within seven calendar days of the majority "yes" challenge vote a freely broadcasted presentation session to last no longer than eight hours, shall broadcast all deliberations and meetings relating to the challenge and shall rule within 30 days of the presentation.

Rationale
Rule and move on, in the public's eye. Traditional cases and proceedings may continue without cameras by the traditional processes in place prior to ratification of this Amendment at the discretion of the court. Arguments given at the presentation session must still be made in the context of the rest of Constitution and prior rulings.

Section 4.
Governors who voted "yes" shall appoint a team to present to the Supreme Court of the United States in the morning session. Governors who

voted "no" shall appoint a team to present in the afternoon session. Each session shall last no longer than 4 hours. Each team may contain members of Congress or their proxies at the team leader's discretion.

Rationale
A fair competition of positions and principles is crucial to the success of the challenge process.

Section 5.
The penalty for a legislator at any level voting for a law that passes but violates a Supreme Court ruling is immediate dismissal from office and permanent forfeiture of eligibility to hold any elected or appointed political office in a local, State or Federal government.

Rationale
This level of accountability has never existed between the governing and the governed. No longer will a politician dismiss the importance of Constitution or their responsibility to preserve, protect and defend it. Constitutional challenges act as the new navigation tool to keep Congress on a path consistent with Constitution. Who better to give this important check to balance the never-ending Federal power grab than the duly elected State leaders?

Our Founders reasoned that frequent citizen elections for the lead positions in Federal government would be a sufficient check on the power of Federal government. They were wrong.

I believe if they saw today's Federal tax code, they'd happily endorse the Constitutional Challenge Amendment and ask just one question, "What took you so long?"

AMENDMENT XXXIII

TECHNOLOGY BRANCH

Section 1.
Because technology plays such a central role in the success of any modern organization, a fourth branch of Federal government, the Technology branch, shall oversee all aspects of technology for the entire Federal government and its sponsored entities.

Rationale
History has shown conclusively that every corner of Federal government having authority over its own technology has created an inefficient and over-priced collection of independent systems (a.k.a. silos) that don't interoperate, don't serve the overall mission and impede Federal government's ability to build, operate and upgrade systems that ultimately serve citizens.

Section 2.
The Technology branch shall respond to requests and contribute unsolicited reports openly to other branches of government and citizens of the country containing analysis on, but not limited to; proposed and existing legislation, existing societal and governmental operational problems, technology opportunities and trends and technology research priorities and progress.

Rationale
It is unrealistic to expect that elected officials have the requisite technological background, expertise or ability to function effectively as leaders of a modern country in the modern world. The Tech branch fills this otherwise ever-widening and evermore damaging gap.

Section 3.
The Technology branch shall be solely responsible to place all dollar amounts in legislation related to technology spending on a line by line basis prior to votes in the U.S. House of Representatives and U.S. Senate.

Rationale
Lobbyists and campaign contributions, related to technology spending, will no longer chase anyone who needs a lot of money to get elected.

Section 4.
The Technology branch shall take steps to move the entire Federal government to become People Interoperable and by oversight authority prevent any action or inaction from undermining the ongoing successful implementation of this objective everywhere throughout Federal government.

Rationale
In a nutshell, People Interoperability (PI) is technology that enables, supports and compels people to work together in ways not possible with even today's most advance computer

systems. Systems certified as People Interoperable contain not just bits and bytes of data left to the skills of human operators to manage, but autonomous information objects that literally need to move where they are needed before they are needed to produce efficiencies and successful results never before dreamed possible from a bureaucracy.

The People Interoperability Model™ originated from research into the complex challenges of emergency response, but applies to day to day operation of any government, company or organization of any size.

Ever lose a file on your computer or the company server? Not any more. Wonder who saw the secret payroll report from Human Resources? Not for long. When will the request for that thing you sent to that department about the person yesterday be complete? A PI system knows. What did they know and when did they know it? The system will be the first place to ask.

See page 54 for more about PI.

Section 5.
The technology branch shall consist of:

Section 5.1.
(2) people appointed by the President of the United States to represent the needs of the executive branch.

Section 5.2.
(1) person appointed by each executive branch cabinet secretary to represent the needs of each department.

Section 5.3.
(9) additional people appointed by Secretary of the Department of Homeland Security to represent the needs of all departments of DHS.

Section 5.4.
(10) people appointed by the Chairman of the Joint Chiefs to represent the needs of the Pentagon.

Section 5.5.
(1) person appointed by each Governor to represent the needs of their State.

Section 5.6.
(1) person appointed by the CEO of each company in the Dow Jones Industrial Average to represent the interests of big business.

Section 5.7.
(3) people appointed by the United States Chamber of Commerce to represent the needs of small business.

Section 5.8.
(2) people appointed by the Administrator of

Charity.gov to represent the needs of non-profits.

Section 5.9.

(10) people appointed by the presidents of the top ten technology universities (as identified by the President of the United States when a representative's term expires).

Rationale

Appointing Technology branch members without advise or consent prevents elections for those positions, campaigning for those positions and the corruption that always accompanies each.

No overlap exists between people who are electable by the public and people who are qualified to serve in the tech branch. Appointments solve that roadblock and fill Federal government with the kind of technology knowledge private companies large and small have wielded to their benefit for decades.

Section 6.

To achieve transparency, all meetings of the Technology branch shall be broadcast and all proposals, recommendations and reservations shall be published on the Internet and made available to all citizens in real-time and by non-expiring archive.

Rationale
Sunlight is the best disinfectant. There is no group better equipped to watch the Tech branch than the typically tech-heavy folks online.

Section 7.
The Technology branch shall specify, design and oversee internal and/or external creation of and use of law making software used by the U.S. House of Representatives and U.S. Senate.

Rationale
The most important software the three branches of Federal government, responsible for securing citizen liberty, must come from and be operated by the most technology savvy people in Federal government.

Section 8.
To improve citizen awareness, education and participation, the Technology branch shall design and oversee implementation and operational maintenance of a nationwide Citizen Voting System that supports citizen voting from everywhere identification can be authenticated (such as but not limited to ATMs, checkout counters, Post Offices, government offices, by mobile device and online). All agencies of Federal government shall be eligible to submit questions for consideration.

Rationale

Encouraging an informed electorate starts by opening the door to have their voice recorded more often. People voting once per week, for example, on a variety of issues can only increase awareness of the issues of the day and the connection society has with one another.

AMENDMENT XXXIV

SYSTEMIC REFORM

Section 1.
The Technology branch shall create and maintain comprehensive system diagrams (CSDs) that define how Federal government interacts with non-governmental civilians.

Rationale
For example: the passport system

Section 2.
The Technology branch shall create and maintain comprehensive system diagrams that define every system that is internal to the operation of Federal government.

Rationale
For example: The General Accounting Office (GAO) audit process

Section 3.
The Technology branch shall create and maintain comprehensive system diagrams that define every system Federal government regulates.

Rationale
For example: The airline industry

Rationale
Creating comprehensive system diagrams for all systems promotes problem solving, debate, analysis, even simulation of proposal impacts. Our modern society repeatedly fails to implement successful systemic reforms in part because we mistakenly never clearly define the problem, never rigorously describe the current system, never meticulously define solutions and never accurately assess consequences.

Section 4.
To promote clarity, transparency and debate, proposals and bills that seek to change, remove from or add to one or more comprehensive system diagrams under control of Federal government shall be openly published (using the law making software) in concert with the plaintext and legislative language of the proposals and bills to clearly document what the comprehensive system diagram(s) would look like if the proposal or bill were implemented.

Rationale
Constructive conversation can only happen when the topic when clarity exists in the minds of all participants. This means the current system diagram must be clear and agreed to as the starting point. Proposed changes to the system must take the form of word and diagram changes. Every citizen has a direct or indirect stake in the operation of any system under Federal control, so access to the current and proposed system diagrams brings transparency

and encourages debate.

While bills only originate from people elected by citizens in Federal elections, section 4 invites proposals from citizens as well as from elected officials.

Section 5.
Systems not under control of Federal government are outside the scope of Federal government's law making and regulatory reach.

Rationale
If government wants the power to legislate operation of a system, then it must assume full responsibility and control of its representation.

Further Notes – Systemic Reform and CSDs
Just passing laws without accepting the requisite responsibility because no one can stop it has led to over 200 years of ever-expanding Federal government control and power. Government extemporaneously deciding its own reach has failed every citizen in virtually every way.

Only when a collection of comprehensive system diagrams (CSDs) appear together can honest, constructive debate regarding the scope of Federal government occur. When a majority of State Governors believe Federal government has over-reached, a Constitutional Challenge can rebalance power.

CSDs contain the following details as blocks (of different shapes, sizes and colors):

- Processes, Inputs, Outputs
- Goods, Services
- Producers, Consumers
- Prices, Taxes
- Money flow, Information flow
- Policies, Laws, Regulations, Punishments

Lines that represent action ("verbs") between two of those components ("nouns") document how they interact. A quick glance at the diagram or simple keyword search reveals, "Consumer pays sales tax." While no single component or action unlocks the mysteries of the universe, all of them together become essential.

A user navigates from page to page and even drills down into more and more layers of system diagrams by simple mouse clicks or finger presses. To see the impacts of a specific reform, another mouse click causes the diagram to reflect the proposed changes. Want to study how did the system worked thirty years ago? No problem.

Industry collected data attaches to system diagrams (even in real time when appropriate) to aid analysis. Exactly how many trauma centers ("producer") are there in the United States? What was their case ("input") and outcome ("outcome") profile last quarter?

Because predictions and forecasts also attach to the boxes and lines, a simple computer operating system creates an execution environment (a sandbox, so to speak) that makes comprehensive system diagrams an economist's new best tool.

Surely everyone wins when everyone involved (especially legislators and voters) first understands how the world operates before trying to reform it with new laws that react (overreact?) to the headline story of the day.

AMENDMENT XXXV

HEALTHCARE

Section 1.

Although it is not an inalienable right, healthcare is a service worthy of equal access to all citizens even in an otherwise free market economy.

Rationale

The financial and social cost (both direct and indirect) of citizens not having proper healthcare is so high that it harms all. A constitutional amendment is the only proper way to recognize healthcare as a service worthy of nationwide equal access.

Section 2.

The Technology branch shall, with tools provided by the Systemic Reform and Law Making amendments, create and maintain operational HealthCare.gov to manage all aspects, including but not limited to scheduling, accounting, malpractice and fraud (detection, prevention and consequences), appointments, test results, diagnoses, treatments, prescriptions, medications, procedures, policies, questions, answers and bookkeeping of the healthcare system throughout the several States.

Healthcare.gov pays all registered healthcare providers in good standing for all products and services rendered in accordance to established best practices.

Rationale
The implementation of Healthcare.gov requires the Technology Branch, Systemic Reform and Law Making amendments to be ratified and fully implemented first. Without the tools and capabilities created by these other Amendments, it would be foolish in the extreme to attempt to devise, much less implement, universal healthcare.

People Interoperability is mandatory for successful implementation of the universal healthcare described in this Amendment.

Centralizing Healthcare.gov assists not only the identification of best practices based on outcomes, but also healthcare provider selection by citizens.

Section 3.
Federal taxes shall fill the National Health Fund for the sole purpose of paying all medical bills to all Healthcare providers in good standing.

Rationale
The overhead (not just profits but operating expenses for the entire insurance industry) to insure is no longer needed and will no longer detract from needed healthcare. Taxes,

premiums and charity pay for everyone's healthcare today, just not efficiently or equally because the system is a hodgepodge of bad ideas poorly executed that cost too much and deliver too little value to too few citizens.

Section 4.

Health insurance of any kind and medical malpractice insurance of any kind shall be prohibited. Healthcare related legislation, regulation, oversight, licensing and agency charters sponsored by Federal government and the several States prior to the ratification of this amendment are hereby repealed and revoked accordingly.

Rationale

Insurance distributes risk and costs across a pool of interest. When the pool is everyone, the overhead of insurance becomes unnecessary. Payments occur via Healthcare.gov. No longer will heath insurance be unnaturally attached to employment.

With Healthcare.gov centralized, redundant inefficiencies throughout the nationwide healthcare system disappear. A medical license functions throughout the nation. The new health clinics operate by the same common set of best practices. The science of medicine although complex, mysterious and often elusive, does not operate by different rules of biology and physics from state to state. The healthcare system will benefit from the same ubiquity once decades-old unnatural constraints of governments vanish.

Section 5.

To focus healthcare provider resources efficiently, a nationwide network of clinics open 24 hours per day, 365 days per year administer to citizens common healthcare needs requiring common procedures safely administered outside hospital and doctor's office. Clinic personnel have access to doctors of all types and specialties for online realtime consultations when needed. Patients referred to a specialist or for a procedure outside the clinic select a provider to their liking using Healthcare.gov.

Rationale

Emergency rooms are for emergency situations and speciality procedures. Clinics are for every day illnesses and common procedures. Doctor's offices are for patients referred by clinics.

Section 6.

Only patients, their family members and freely chosen accredited healthcare professionals in good standing shall make medical decisions.

Rationale

Healthcare decisions won't be made by companies, laws, regulations, politicians or political appointees because none of them have the mission or means to deliver quality results. Providing routine inexpensive medical care by the most expensive means (emergency rooms) mostly ceases when a network of high quality clinics becomes available.

Section 7.

Because treatment is not the only important facet of healthcare, Healthcare.gov shall promote incentives to reward citizens' healthy actions. It shall create, publish and oversee use of online and offline materials to achieve health education throughout the citizenry.

Rationale
Spending a smart dollar on prevention can save a tragic thousand dollars of treatment.

Section 8.

Accredited healthcare professionals shall join Healthcare.gov to make their services available and their results produced freely known to the public. Advertising by healthcare provider members of Healthcare.gov other than signage on the property where their services are rendered shall be prohibited. Delivering medical services by anyone not a member in good standing of Healthcare.gov shall be prohibited.

Rationale
Every healthcare provider in good standing benefits from the same exposure in Healthcare.gov, which links services available and results produced. Every citizen benefits from online access to searchable, unfiltered,

identity–free results by condition, disease and treatment.

Healthcare providers must compete on results, not price, sales incentives, reimbursements or fancy wasteful advertising.

AMENDMENT XXXVI

MONOPOLY COMPENSATION

Section 1.

When Federal government with just cause and after due process assigns monopoly standing to a company in an industry, all related goods and services from said company shall be made available to Federal government and governments of and in the several States at cost, excluding research, development and overhead, in the name of the citizens of the country.

Rationale

Since every monopoly itself (although not the monopoly exploiter) is owned implicitly and collectively by all citizens of the country, it stands to reason that all citizens deserve compensation when a company's market dominance evolves into a monopoly. Although courts decide (on behalf of citizens) to allow a company to be the monopoly provider or engage in monopolistic practices, it comes with consequences due to all citizens. The company is allowed to profit from the monopoly, but it must no longer expect to also profit from payments derived by taxes from the same people who own the monopoly in the first place!

For example, if government allows a software company to maintain a monopoly and/or engage in monopolistic practices, government gets that company's software for only the cost of pressing CDs or downloading files as necessary as compensation for the privilege to operate as a monopoly. In this example compensation due to the citizenry for exploitation of that monopoly comes in the form of the citizens' governments running more efficiently and costing less money.

AMENDMENT XXXVII

FACILITATION

Section 1.
Because facilitating charity, not forced redistribution, is a proper role of government, the Technology branch shall create and maintain operational Charity.gov to facilitate matching those with means and those with needs.

Rationale
Forced redistribution is a magnet for corruption and the life blood of the always dysfunctional and often harmful runaway nanny state.

Section 2.
Effective April 15th the year following ratification of this Amendment, the Federal corporate income tax rate shall be zero and all laws, regulations, tax codes, tax credits and rules relating to Federal corporate income tax shall be null and void; all agencies, departments, groups and organizations relating to Federal corporate income tax shall be disbanded.

Rationale
Companies don't really pay taxes. The amount they aren't able to shelter with loopholes and costly tax tricks is simply collected from customers via higher prices.

Section 3.
For-profit companies of all types with an address anywhere in the United States or its territories shall pay monthly a flat tax, without exemptions, credits, waivers or loopholes of any kind, on their liquid assets regardless of location or form. This shall be the only financial burden Federal government may impose on, extract from or compel of for-profit companies.

Rationale
Putting money to work helps the economy more than hoarding it does. Hiding money offshore, overseas, in other companies, in shells or off the books no longer cheats everyone from the benefits of tax revenue.

Section 4.
Congress shall by law each January set the corporate flat tax rate to begin the following January and continue for the entire calendar year without possibility of change. Failure to do so shall leave the previous rate in place for the entire year.

Rationale
RationalePredictability and stability are positive market forces that contribute to a healthy business and employment climate and a healthy economy.

Section 5.
Individuals with means shall direct their one-time and/or ongoing cash and goods contributions

to Charity.gov to charities of their choice and reduce their Federal tax burden dollar for dollar.

Rationale

The nanny state that redistributes wealth not only services those in need the least efficient way possible - which denies others in need - but also it allows citizens to overlook their civic and patriotic duty to voluntarily be charitable. Charity is a value to hold dear, not to hide behind a bureaucracy.

Section 6.

Non-profit organizations shall use Charity.gov in real-time to account for all activities monetary and non-monetary to achieve complete transparency to all citizens.

Rationale

Non-profit organizations act on behalf of all citizens and thus are accountable to all citizens.

Section 7.

Only non-profits who continually produce a track record of positive results and low administrative overhead shall be eligible for distributions from Charity.gov.

Rationale

Reward success. Punish failure.

Section 8.

Charity.gov shall publish online in realtime contributions and distributions of all types to and from all parties.

Rationale

Complete transparency reveals fraud, prevents misinformation and informs consumers.

Section 9.

Congress shall determine and make public by law minimum charitable giving thresholds required for corporations to become eligible to do business with Federal government.

Rationale

Profiting from doing business with the People's government comes with a social price tag, not with a ticket to ride an unrestricted gravy train.

NEXT STEPS

There is a saying I coined in the 1980's during my days in the telecommunication industry, "In the history of the world, a standards document has never processed a telephone call." The main idea is simply this; words on a page no matter how wise, remain unsatisfying until someone takes action to give them life. Consider these actions.

Step 1.

Boldly ask yourself, "What kind of country do I want to live in?" Paint a picture in your head so clear that every day you see the differences between what we have and what you want, especially when you consume the news of the day and follow politics.

It is one thing to be unhappy about what the government is doing, to be against this or that policy or proposal, to pick up a sign and protest; it's another to know what principles you deeply believe, passionately promote and vigorously defend.

Step 2.

"Gather your patriots."

Find the people in your circle of friends and family who have any interest in politics or government – even when it's not election or tax time.

Step 3.

For people with no active interest, but who like to read, lend them a spare copy of this book then gauge their interest in discussing it.

Step 4.

Meet periodically and start an email group to discuss the events of the day in context of the principles in The Next 10 Amendments.

Step 5.

Ask people in your local area their opinions about the principles, especially business and political leaders and candidates.

Step 6.

Share these ideas with children! Even if it takes fifty years for one of these Amendments to emerge, one of your children could be the one to pick up the mantle and lead the way.

Step 7.

Search for The Next 10 Amendments app for your smartphone or tablet. Installing those plugs you into the emerging community of like-minded patriots.

PEOPLE INTEROPERABILITY

The Technology Branch Amendment commissions the newly minted Tech Branch to implement People Interoperability throughout Federal government. As the inventor of this concept, I know a brief introduction will help.

In the wake of the attacks of 9/11/2001, one truth transitioned from tragic story to a lesson learned to a call to action very quickly, "In an emergency, First Responders must be able to communicate with each other." In a nutshell, different agencies from different jurisdictions used different communication systems that were not compatible, which made communication on 9/11 a deadly mess. In the parlance of the day, we lacked "interoperability."

That's all true, but, unfortunately, it's not enough. My homeland security research (using some of the same techniques that led me to the Amendments and to invent a new kind of Exchange Traded Fund) revealed that what everyone (and I mean everyone in the homeland security industry, worldwide) calls interoperability, is really only telecommunications interoperability.

The actual problem to solve is much larger and more complex than conventional wisdom acknowledges. Anyone who has worked anywhere near the government understands implicitly that conventional wisdom drives decision making which leads to billions of dollars of spending. The dirty mantra that has driven the military industrial complex for decades is,

"What the government is willing to pay for trumps what they really need." That's a bleak portrait, but before I tell you the bright side, here is the heart of the solution, my People Interoperability Model.™

People Interoperability Model™

Team	17. People
	16. Mission

Behavior	15. Tasking & Schedule
	14. Resources
	13. Authority
	12. Location Awareness
	11. Skill & Capability
	10. Procedure & Process
	9. Policy

Active Info	8. Automated Notification
	7. Subscription
	6. Query
	5. Permission
	4. Evolving Information
	3. Language

™ Comm	2. Transmit & Receive
	1. Connectivity

First the good news, telecom interoperability, the thing everyone is building that they think solves the entire problem, is level 1 and 2 of the whole problem. This means, the billions of dollars spent since 9/11 to "make all the radios work together" is money well spent, as long as the other 15 levels follow!

Now for the really good news, the nuts and bolts of each level including how to implement People Interoperability in a nationwide 9 year plan throughout every level of domestic homeland security is beyond the scope of this book, so I won't bore you with the details. Just know that the People Interoperability Model™ improves the way systems are designed, software is built, information is managed and people work together. Not since the middle of the 1970's has Computer Science offered such a game-changing inflection point.

You might be wondering (if you are still actually reading this chapter) if solving a specific homeland security problem rises to the level of a Constitutional Amendment. That's a fair question worthy of debate, until you consider the following unintended consequence.

Look back for a moment at the words used for each level of the People Interoperability Model.™ None of those words have anything to do with homeland security itself. I started out to solve a homeland security problem after I realized in horror during Katrina that my industry had not helped government solve its emergency response deficiencies. But the breakthroughs came quickly when I realized that equipment working together isn't the proper objective, people working together is.

That led to the insight that makes People Interoperability an imperative for a modern nation. The challenge of people interoperating exists everywhere a group of people exists as a natural consequence of people being people. The challenge is as much social as technical; it's as much about ego as software; it's as much about identity as gadgets. The result of People Interoperability applied to homeland security is a vision unimaginable by conventional means:

"When a public crisis hits, facts, issues, questions, answers, decisions, tasks, resources, requests, plans, and procedures all represented as data, text, voice, images and video travel to and from any number of people and places; needs to be captured, shared, update and corrected; needs to be coordinated across multiple agencies in multiple jurisdictions with a precision, predictability and confidence as though this exact group of first responders address this exact crisis every single day; no matter the scale and even if the incident has never been considered."

Outside homeland security, the message is also clear. Every organization with more than a few people or that interacts with an organization with more than a few people needs People Interoperable technology (not just old fashioned software "tools") to help accomplish its objectives cheaply, quickly and with high quality.

Sounds like every nook and cranny of Federal government to me! And therefore, it is worthy of mention in the Constitutional Amendment that creates the branch of government capable of implementation.

When Federal government operates more efficiently than the private sector at large, it will be a great day in human history. It sounds crazy and impossible, because it is crazy and impossible with the current state of the art tools, techniques, technology and thinking. However, improve all the inputs and the outputs will improve too.

There's another principle at work here worth highlighting. I believe one of the primary roles of any government is to lead by example. Imagine what the country might be like if leading by example were as enshrined from the start as concepts such as "unalienable rights," "checks and balances," "separation of church and state," and "law making." Imagine if our Founders coined the term "examplemaker" to complement politicians' role as lawmaker.

Some believe "government is as government demands." While plenty of history exists to support that conventional wisdom, imagine if first and foremost "government is as government does."

Imagine if before a government passed a law mandating truthful labels on a company's products, they implemented truthful claims about their legislation (see the Law Making Amendment).

Imagine if every problem politicians tried to solve by passing laws to govern other people, they actually solved inside government first.

Imagine if a politician lying to the public carried the same penalty as a citizen lying to government.

Imagine if making examples was as rewarding as making laws.

Leading by example spreads the best solutions very quickly, faster than making demands.

By my way of thinking, those governing owe it to those governed to lead by example and to repeatedly earn the privilege to wield the sacred power entrusted to them. Passing laws should not be the objective, solving problems should.

Here's to that future of a more perfect union!

CITIZEN CONSTITUTIONAL CONVENTION™

Some people believe that the importance of Constitution diminishes the further you get from Washington D.C. After all, don't we hire all those politicians to worry about Constitution and laws and stuff so we don't have to? No, not really.

The U.S. Constitution is the people's constitution. Washington D.C. is not the United States. Citizens are the United States. Constitution is our document to protect and defend... and yes, to amend. Even if you disagree with every principle, every idea, every amendment, every concept, and every proposal in this book, you simply can't hide from one immutable truth – government works for citizens. Government rules citizens only because citizens loan people in government authority to rule.

With that in mind, I'm proud to announce, coming to a hotel ballroom or school gymnasium (or an empty field if necessary) near you the Citizen Constitutional Convention™. It is beyond unrealistic to the point of folly to expect or believe a majority of politicians in Washington D.C. will, on their own, of their own mind come to the conclusion, "Hey, let's put the country on the path that will lead to success for the next 100 years and adopt The Next 10 Amendments." 100 years? Find a politician who can say with a straight face that their event horizon is more than 100 days and I'll show you a politician you should run from, quickly.

That's okay. We need not be limited by anyone's lack of vision. After all did our Founders believe that the box British rule constructed for them bounded their destiny? Of course not. We just need D.C. to pay attention to us when we show them where we're going. Once they believe enough of us believe, they'll step up, scurry around and fall all over themselves to lead us there. After all, for all the governing skill our modern political system lacks, no shortage of campaign science exists to get politicians elected.

All this points to one thing, a Constitutional Convention. Not a bunch of politicians with pensions and campaigns and backsides, I mean legacies, to protect. Citizens. Citizens of all backgrounds and beliefs, of all persuasions and principles. gathering all over the country. Citizens who realize that which is most important of all, the country, is at stake come together to discuss, debate, ponder, project, predict, listen, learn, question, challenge, compromise, create and craft a vision of the future so clear and so compelling as to demand attention from other citizens – even those who never thought themselves political.

A Citizen Constitutional Convention™.

Citizen Constitutional Convention™ - Act I
Copyright 2013 Dan Farfan

FADE IN:

INT. NIGHT. ENTRANCE TO HIGH SCHOOL

We see an 8 foot folding table set up at the entrance of a long
hallway with upper and lower lockers on each side. About half way
down the hall people mill about, chatting, drinking and snacking
on finger foods. Bulletin boards decorate each side of entrance to
what clearly is "Home of the Celts." BOB BERENDZEN enters
somewhat timidly.

> BOB BERENDZEN
> Hello, this is my first time. I think
> I'm in the right place.

> HOSTESS
> (friendly)
> Why yes. You certainly are. Welcome.

HOSTESS hands BOB a two part registration card. One half for
his information and the other for his name tag.

> HOSTESS
> Just fill this out, darlin' then the
> name part goes in here. First name
> only. Write it big so it's easy to
> read.

HOSTESS points to a plastic holder with a string that clearly goes
around the neck - like the one she's wearing. BOB follows
directions, places it around his neck.

> BOB BERENDZEN
> (pointing towards the people)

```
I'm guessing it's that way?
```

                    HOSTESS
                   (jokingly)
```
Yep. That's why we put the food
there. Enjoy!
```

BOB makes his way slowly toward the people, with a sense of
anticipation of the unknown.

               BOB BERENDZEN
                 (to himself)
```
What am I doing here? If this is a
waste of time, Zamberlan is going to
get an earful.
```

Now where the hallway opens to a large cafeteria lunch room,
BOB scans the food table before heading toward to the auditorium.

                     LAURA
                (from behind BOB)
```
First timer?
```

               BOB BERENDZEN
                  (startled)
```
What? Oh yes. Me? Yes.
```

Monosyllabic words is all BOB can muster.

                     LAURA
```
Good. Welcome. I'm Laura. Trust me on
this. Don't be too quick to come to
any conclusions. Take it all in
tonight.
```

                     LAURA
               (hands BOB a flyer)

Take this and see you later to chat.
Okay?

BOB BERENDZEN
(takes the flyer)

Sure.

A little thrown off by what just happened, BOB makes his way to a seat middle of the 30 or so rows of seats on the left side, outside aisle. A comfortable place for him in a room of about 50 people. BOB reads the flyer:

BOB BERENDZEN
(to himself)

Agenda: Hour 1: B.I.R. Background,
Introduction, Review by Facilitator,
Recorder, Timekeeper. 10 minute break
before Hour 2... Wow, if a group this
large can maintain a schedule this
closely it'll be a miracle.

BOB notices a QUIK code on the flyer but before he has a chance to scan it with his smart phone he hears a voice at the back of the room where he entered

MATT WOODS
(loudly to the people in the lunch room)

Hello. Everyone. We'll be starting in
5 minutes so please take a seat.
Thanks.

BOB BERENDZEN
(to himself, smiling)

Five minutes til. Very prompt. That's
a good start.

His attention back on the handout, BOB realizes the QUIK code leads to a smartphone app (Android AND iPhone).

BOB BERENDZEN
(to himself)
Okay. These folks have a custom app.
Interesting. But is it worthwhile or
a colossal waste of time?

BOB's smartphone vibrates. A text from his friend CHRIS
ZAMBERLAN. "Don't be to quick to come to any conclusions.
Take it all in."

BOB BERENDZEN
(types reply message into phone)
"That's strange. Same thing Laura
said to me."

CHRIS ZAMBERLAN
(text message)
"Oh good. You met Laura. Her and
husband Keith are great. Enjoy B.I.R.
I'll be there in 1 hour."

BOB BERENDZEN
(text message)
"OK, but the crab puff looking things
will likely be gone by then ;-)"

CHRIS ZAMBERLAN
(text message)
"NP. Not crab. lol"

BOB shakes his head. Fooled by finger food, again! MATT takes
the stage.

MATT WOODS
(at a mic on a stand)
"Hello everyone. Thanks for coming to
this meeting of the Citizen
Constitutional Convention™!"

Applause fills the room. BOB joins in politely.

> ## MATT WOODS
> My name is MATT WOODS. I'm the facilitator of this group. If you ever have any questions or problems almost everyone you meet tonight can help, but the buck stops right here. I look forward to meeting all the new people. If I don't find you later, please find me. This first hour is the Background, Introduction and Review - what we call BIR for short.

> ## BOB BERENDZEN
> (to himself, smiling)
> Never let the chance for a good acronym go to waste.

> ## MATT WOODS
> You'll meet our Timekeeper, Dean Shillito and Secretary, John Voda, in a few minutes after I finish the Background and Introduction.

MATT shows the audience a book from his pocket

> ## MATT WOODS
> Here it is. The book that started it all, "The Next 10 Amendments," written by a Computer Scientist named Dan Farfan in 2010. Dan is the kind of person whose brain doesn't stop. He once spent 6 months, full time, devising from a blank sheet a paper an entire education system. Not a school, an education *system* built on six simple but powerful principles.

And this not just words and theories on paper, but also massive spreadsheet that nails down every dollar from the cost to construct the buildings to the price of a meal in the cafeteria. I haven't seen the 50 page white paper that resulted - almost no one has yet - but he tells me, and I believe him, that following his plan, K-12 school would be free for all students in the United States in just 40 years AND free from any government connection whatsoever.

> BOB BERENDZEN
> (to himself)

Huh?

> MATT WOODS

Dan once spent 6 weeks writing a screenplay to demonstrate that Microsoft's best move in the 90's when pressured by the U.S. Justice Department would've been to change domiciles.

> MATT WOODS

It's important to understand about Dan that he doesn't believe in no government. He believes in no *bad* government. He believes when government does what government shouldn't be doing, bad government is the only possible result.

> BOB BERENDZEN
> (to himself, impressed)

That's for sure.

MATT WOODS

Dan believes that bad government is
our fault - citizens - not
politicians or pundits, not lobbyists
or ideologues, not campaign
consultants or commentators; it's our
fault.

MATT WOODS

Dan believes that the bigger the
problem the more attention it
deserves. The problems most people
run from, Dan takes up residence.
Dan's three U.S. patents create a
solution to one of the most annoying
accidental by-products of the
telephony world, being put on hold.
Something everyone takes for granted
as simply terrible that must always
be terrible. Not so. Unfortunately
one of his former employers, maybe
you've heard of them, **AT&T**, owns
those and choses not to commercialize
them.

BOB BERNEDZEN
(to himself, shock)

Seriously?

MATT WOODS

The content in this book is entirely
original and came in little pieces
over 30 years. Every time, since the
80's - Dan has been online since
before the Internet was called
Internet - when an answer to an
online question or when posting a
message of any consequence online,

Dan kept a copy. Eventually, the ideas jelled. The principles coalesced and ten Amendments to the U.S. Constitution rose to the top.

BOB BERENDZEN
(to himself, in awe)
30 years? I don't even know what I was doing 30 years ago.

MATT WOODS
(reading from the book)
Being a fellow tech guy, the passage that first impressed me is from the introduction, *"my background allows me too look at the United States of America as a giant, but finite, system of complex systems. My respect for the subject matter allows me to accept Constitution as the proper place where systemic fixes belong. My analysis techniques, a particularly geeky subject for another time, fortunately do not muddle the output offered in the following pages. I provide with each Amendment a simple rationale that places the solution in the context of familiar problems and often not so familiar principles."*

MATT WOODS
(admiration)
".. look at the United States as a giant, but finite, system of complex systems." I love that phrase. If you haven't read the book yet, pick up a copy and you'll agree with me it

provides a fantastic foundation for
our mission.

MATT WOODS

Which brings us to the Introduction.
Given all that, what are we doing
here? What is the CCC, really? We all
know what Constitution is. Most of us
have some vague notion of what a
Constitutional Convention is, or was
from the past. But most people, I
know this was true for me until
recently, most people think of these
things in abstract terms. It is the
easiest thing in the world to take
for granted that which we've always
had that requires no work. How much
does a child who has lived in a
comfortable home with 3 meals a day
on the kitchen table take for granted
that home and those meals?
Completely. They've always had it.
They don't necessarily do anything to
earn it, so they come to the
conclusion, in the face of no
evidence to the contrary that what
they have is how it is for everyone.
It's just how things are.

MATT WOODS

But we aren't children. We cannot
take for granted that government or
the country will keep working in the
future because it has always worked
in the past. We know better than
that. Government needs our help. They

are so busy doing what they do,
campaigning in the next election...

laughter

BOB BERENDZEN
(to himself)

I like this Matt guy.

MATT WOODS

... even if they just won an
election... they are so busy with the
machinery that is government that
they have no time to ponder the
future. Any by future I don't mean
the next year or five or ten. I mean
the next 100 years, 200 years. Our
Founders gave us a document that put
everyone on a path that got us here.
What will we have to say to the folks
who are around 200 years from now?
Sorry? We couldn't think of any new
ideas? Sorry? We didn't learn
anything at all from the first 237
years, so it's up to you? Sorry? I
heard the rallying cry ".. in order
to form a more perfect Union" but I
didn't think it meant me?

MATT WOODS

I don't know about you, but that's
simply not good enough for me. The
CCC is our chance in our time to give
a gift of clarity, of wisdom, of love
to future generations, so that they
can do the same instead of struggle
with the 300 year old foundation that
hasn't been touched much or

challenged much or been strengthened much.

So, what have we learned? What's gone wrong in government? What can we do to improve the country for all citizens by improving the foundation of it all, the U.S. Constitution?

The book is the start of the conversation and debate and disagreement and, and, and... Dean and John will talk about that in a few minutes.

MATT WOODS
Our two objectives are pretty straightforward, which is not to say they are simple: One, Reach consensus on Amendment language to bring forward to the next level CCC - namely, the State CCC meetings. And secondly, to eventually elect delegates to send to that next level to represent the work we've done here.

BOB BERENDZEN
(to himself, shocked)
Next level? Delegates? These people are not fooling around.

MATT WOODS
There is a quote I like to end my part of the Introduction with because to me it captures one of the most important concepts everyone must keep in mind so that CCC succeeds.

Up on the big screen, a picture of that quote engraved into the wall of the inner chamber of the Lincoln Memorial.

MATT WOODS

"Never doubt that a small group of thoughtful, committed citizens can change the world; indeed, it's the only thing that ever has." Margaret Mead.

MATT WOODS

We are that small group of thoughtful, committed citizens. We are not alone. This meeting is happening in many cities large and small all over the country tonight, in fact, every night - using exactly this agenda, using the same book as the foundation, using the same mobile app ... and if you don't have that yet installed, I suggest you get it during the 10 minute break before hour 2 begins. It's brilliant. It's the only way to keep connected. It's free if you just want to follow along with the group's progress. It's just a few bucks if you want to contribute. And please, know that we want everyone to contribute.

And now, here is our Secretary, John Voda.

JOHN VODA bounds to the stage with high energy

JOHN VODA

Let's hear it for Matt. Thanks for being our facilitator. Without

leadership, all that would be left is
chaos.

My part of the introduction was added
because early CCC meetings often
became unnecessarily confusing
because while it's good that we all
come from different backgrounds,
where we must come together is
Constitution. We aren't all lawyers
and scholars and judges, so a primer,
a set of ground rules for content was
created. Here it is.

Since this list in his handout BOB reads along with JOHN and
notices that already, just from this simple set of content guidelines,
he's already learned something about Constitution.

JOHN VODA

1) Constitution doesn't mandate
citizen behavior or punish citizen
misbehavior. That's what laws do.
Some people think that what's in
Constitution are just the most
important laws. This is not the
case. My favorite example is the
Second Amendment. It enumerates
the right to bare arms. It doesn't
say citizens must own guns. That
some don't in no way diminishes
the value of the right that all
have.

2) Constitution protects citizen and
States rights from government
overreach by being the framework
for liberty. Liberty means the
right to make choices.

3) Constitution enumerates rights automatically conferred to humans, not by government, but by nature, the universe, the Creator, however you chose to attribute the source of all things. Thus, phrases such as "Constitution gives the right to..." completely miss the mark. Life gives rights to humans, not government, not people, not documents.

4) Constitution establishes the basic structure and operation of Federal government.

BOB BERENDZEN
(to himself)

Oh, now this is my favorite of all. Well done.

JOHN VODA

5) Constitution spells out checks and balances among the branches of government.

JOHN VODA

So what good does this list do us? This is the list against which all proposed content us compared. If something doesn't match at least one of these, chances are it doesn't belong in Constitution -- or at least not as stated.

Consider it a sanity check to keep us from going off the rails and doing

something ill advised such as a
balanced budget Amendment.

JOHN VODA

And now, if there are no questions
<pause>... it's my pleasure to
introduce Dean Shillito, our
timekeeper.

DEAN SHILLITO

Hello everyone. So great to see so
many new faces. I'll be quick. Just
as there are ground rules for content
eligible for Constitution, there are
ground rules for our behavior during
CCC meetings.

1) Treat people with respect (No
   interrupting, yelling at people,
   name calling or personal attacks
   for example)

2) Stay on topic

3) No logical fallacies or info
   tricks

BOB BERENDZEN
(to himself)

These are good rules. But my pet
peeve is...

DEAN SHILLITO

4) And for everyone's sanity, please,
   side conversations more than a
   couple of whispered sentences
   belong outside only.

BOB BERENDZEN
(to himself)
Wow. That's it. Seems these folks
know how to run a meeting!

5) Finally, when you want to
participate in the discussion, raise
your hand. When the leader gives you
the floor you stand, add your two
cents and STAY STANDING until the
current discussion is over.

It's my job to jump in when any of
these rules are broken. For the
benefit of the whole group, follow
the rules. The only sanction after a
warning is removal. Multiple removals
can lead to exile.

MATT WOODS
Thanks John and Dean. Now, part 2 of
this first hour, the Review. Here is
an overview of the ground we've
covered...

Up on the big screen, slide after slide summarize, per Amendment
discussions, debates and majority rule conclusions. Even a few
original contributions for new Amendments fly by.

MATT WOODS
Of course I encourage everyone new to
access the archive available in the
mobile app. This is an overview, but
you can drill down to see real detail
on any of these topics. It's all in
there because it's all important. We

learn something from even our
missteps.

BOB BERENDZEN
(to himself)
Did he just acknowledge mistakes?

A proposed Amendment on the big screen now.

MATT WOODS
(sad, regretful)
This is one that still haunts me,
frankly. I know some of you were here
the night this went down. To make a
long story short, there was a
citizen, in your seats, who had been
coming to CCC for quite a while. He
was 20-something. Extremely
personable. I didn't know anyone who
didn't like him. Articulate. And
analytical. He could listen to a
debate on a concept, no matter its
complexity, and contribute just a few
sentences that got right to the heart
of the issue, sometimes even adding
clarity for both sides, at the same
time!

BOB BERENDZEN
(to himself)
Geez, did this guy die?

MATT WOODS
And then came the night he proposed
an original Amendment. That's when
the wheels came off, so to speak. Not
everyone agreed, which is to be
expected. We debated the issues as

we're supposed to. It was civil
enough. But in the end, he took the
challenge from the opposition very,
very personally. Even though these
things can take many sessions to
hammer out, revise, rewrite, trim,
revisit, etc. he lost interest in
CCC. Far too soon.

MATT WOODS

Here's my regret. I talked to him
afterwards and thanked him for
bringing something so creative. He
mentioned he wished everyone agreed
with me, and him. And I said without
thinking, "Everyone's not that
creative." I meant it to compliment
him, but what he heard must've been
something like, "That has no chance
in this group." We haven't seen him
since.

MATT WOODS

We lost a valuable member that night
and maybe if I had made it clear to
him that his contribution is valuable
to us all, maybe if I had reminded
him that opposition doesn't mean
defeat, maybe if I had reminded him
that sometimes when people don't
agree, they just don't agree, yet.
Maybe we'd still have him with us.
That's a lesson I learned the hard
way.

BOB tries to recall the last time he's witnessed a leader admit a
mistake and so eloquently state an accurate lesson learned.

BOB BERENDZEN
(to himself, impressed)
Never seen that before.

MATT moves to a different part of the stage. Big screen changes to a different Amendment

MATT WOODS
(changing volume, pitch, energy)
I like to end the review with this open item. Another original Amendment that's still being considered, refined, etc. It's not on the schedule for tonight. We're waiting for indication from the originators, Laura and Keith that they are ready to dazzle us.

LAURA
(jokingly, out loud)
... again ...

laughter

MATT WOODS
Yes, of course. Dazzle us *again*.

BOB BERENDZEN
(to himself, smiling)
Cute.

MATT WOODS
Okay, that's the BIR. Are there any questions I can answer before we take a break until the top of the hour? ...

KYLE PACE raises his hand

MATT WOODS

Yes?

KYLE PACE

Someone in line in front of me paid
the dues. How many government
agencies, besides the IRS, were
informed when she swiped her credit
card?

laughter.

MATT WOODS

Ahhh.. the big question these days.
How many agencies will audit me
because I came to a CCC meeting? Let
me be blunt. I have no idea what
snooping Federal government does via
internet or financial companies or
anything. However, I can tell you
this, we are not non-profit. Payments
or contributions of cash or donuts or
appetizers or a bag of fruit are not
tax deductible.

MATT WOODS

I wasn't in the room at the time, but
I'm told that when asked about why
being a for-profit entity was a
requirement to purchase the statewide
rights to operate CCC meetings, Dan
Farfan said, "Simple. I'm a
capitalist. Anything worth doing is
worth doing well. If we need tax
breaks or handouts from anyone not in

the room, we're doing too bad of a
job to be allowed to continue."

                BOB BERENDZEN
                  (to himself)
Purchased? Statewide rights? These
people are serious.

                KYLE PACES
Thank you, Matt. Good answer.

                MATT WOODS
Okay everyone. Back in 12 minutes for
Hour 2.

FADE OUT:

Citizen Constitutional Convention™ - Act II
Copyright 2013 Dan Farfan

FADE IN:

INT. NIGHT. LUNCH ROOM

BOB made his way back to the lunch room. It's 70% full of people. Approximately 150 people greeting, chatting, catching up.

> BOB BERENDZEN
> (to himself)
> Wow. More people than I would've guessed. And everyone pulled away from network primetime television. Maybe there is hope...

From behind a surprise grab on the shoulders.

> CHRIS ZAMBERLAN
> (joking)
> Are you a patriot or a red coat?

> BOB BERENDZEN
> (mockingly ready to throw down and battle)
> I'm both. What's it to you?

> CHRIS ZAMBERLAN
> Great to see you. Glad you made it. What did you think of the BIR? Glad you came? What's up?

> BOB BERENDZEN
> First of all, no more pastries for you. That was about 5 questions. It was good. I was impressed.

CHRIS ZAMBERLAN
I told you these folks are the real
deal, right?

BOB BERENDZEN
Well, we'll see. I'm glad you invited
me though.

CHRIS ZAMBERLAN
Great. Great. Great. Did you install
the mobile app, yet?

BOB BERENDZEN
No. I'll get it later. I was just
going to find Laura or Keith. Matt
mentioned they are working on an
original Amendment. I want to know
more about it.

CHRIS ZAMBERLAN
Everyone does. Let's find them.

CHRIS and BOB make their way through the crowd. Several
people greet CHRIS. CHRIS introduces BOB. A few times until...

MATT WOODS
Okay everyone. Let's find a seat so
we can start on time in 4 minutes.

CHRIS ZAMBERLAN
No worries. We'll chat with them
after the meeting. The building stays
open until midnight.

BOB BERENDZEN
Let's get a good seat.

CHRIS smiles to himself - glad to see such excitement in his friend over something so important. Like clockwork, the crowd is seated and ready to go on time.

> MATT WOODS
> Thanks for coming everyone – and on
> time. Makes me feel like Mussolini
> with all my little trains on time.

semi-laughter and semi-groan from the audience.

> MATT WOODS
> This is the night I've been most
> anxious for and I know many of you
> have been too. The Technology Branch.
> Dan proposes literally adding a 4th
> branch to Federal govt.

> BOB BERENDZEN
> (whispers to Chris)
>
> Seriously?

> CHRIS ZAMBERLAN
> (whispers)
> Yep. That's why you had to come
> tonight. This is epic.

> MATT WOODS
> Since this is our first night
> treating this Amendment, there is no
> catchup to bridge the gap between
> where last meeting left off and this
> meeting starts, so let's just dive
> right in. Who wants to volunteer to
> read the sections?

A 40-something pretty Italian pops out of her seat with the energy of a teenager, her hand raised.

> ANGELA TESTA
I will, Matt.

> MATT WOODS
Excellent. Thanks Angela. Okay and who for the rationale?

Another hand goes up

> MARK COUGHLIN
> (jokingly)
Can I do an accent??

laughter

> MATT WOODS
> (faking displeasure)
Only if you have a good one now.

more laughter.

> MATT WOODS
Okay we're set. For those of you following along in the book. We go section 1, then its rationale. Then section 2 and so on. After the reading comes Q&A, the proposals, then debate, then we recap item by item. Any questions.

silence. MATT taps a few times on his tablet computer to display on the screen the text of Section 1 and Rationale 1.

> MATT WOODS
Take us there, Angela and Mark.

ANGELA TESTA

Amendment 23. Technology Branch.
Because technology plays such a
central role in the success of any
modern organization, a fourth branch
of Federal government, the Technology
branch, shall oversee all aspects of
technology for the entire Federal
government and its sponsored
entities.

MARK COUGHLIN

Rationale 1. History has shown
conclusively that every corner of
Federal government having authority
over its own technology has created
an inefficient and over-priced
collection of independent systems
(aka silos) that don't interoperate,
don't serve the overall mission and
impede Federal government's ability
to build, operate and upgrade systems
and ultimately serve citizens.

BOB BERENDZEN
(whispers to CHRIS)

That's all true, but growing
government can't help.

CHRIS ZAMBERLAN
(whispers)

Just wait. You'll see.

As it was read, section after section each with its own rationale that completely made sense to BOB, he becomes more visibly excited and barely able to keep himself in his seat. The reading of the Amendment comes to an end.

MATT WOODS
Let's hear it for Angela and Mark!
Well done.

applause. BOB jumps up out of his seat.

BOB BERENDZEN
(unable to contain himself)
Matt, I'm sorry to interrupt. I know
I'm new here and I don't really know
how this part of the meeting flows,
but I just gotta say, as a life-long
Computer Scientist, I've never heard
anything smarter in my life. The Tech
Branch is *exactly* what government
needs.

MATT WOODS
Excellent. Thanks for the
enthusiastic appraisal. Dan Farfan is
a Computer Scientist too. I'm sure
he'd be happy to hear you agree. Be
sure to enter that feedback into the
mobile app. Everyone, look for it
later. Let's vote .. um.. what's your
name?

BOB BERENDZEN
I'm Bob Berendzen

MATT WOODS
Everyone, let's vote Bob's feedback
up so it gets forwarded to Dan.
Thanks Bob.

BOB sits down. MATT taps a button or two on his tablet computer
to display section 1 on the big screen.

MATT WOODS
Okay. I see there are 3 questions
about section 1. Let's dive right in.

BOB BERENDZEN
(whispers to CHRIS)
Where did the questions come from?

CHRIS ZAMBERLAN
(whispers)
All from people here in the local
chapter. Mostly entered before the
meeting, because they have the book
and the app.. and want some things
clarified.

BOB BERENDZEN
(impressed)
Awesome. People *prepared* for the
meeting. I wish everyone on my
development team did that.

CHRIS ZAMBERLAN
I hear ya.

Section by section, questions are answered one by one, until..

MATT WOODS
Oh great, an open vote. "How
concerned are you that growing the
size of Federal government with Tech
Branch will ultimately do more harm
than good?"

BOB BERENDZEN
(to CHris)
What? No way.

The audience shuffles to grab for their mobile device to weigh in on the open vote.

> ### BOB BERENDZEN
> (to Chris)

What's happening?

> ### CHRIS ZAMBERLAN

Everyone gets to vote via the mobile app... well, paid members that is.

> ### BOB BERENDZEN

How much does it cost?

> ### CHRIS ZAMBERLAN

To save democracy and put the Country on a sustainable path for the next 200 years? Less than you spend on coffee in a day.

> ### BOB BERENDZEN

Really?

> ### CHRIS ZAMBERLAN

But the cool thing is that along with the questions and answers and feedback and proposals and debates, the open votes from all the chapters all over the country go into a common database so they can be analyzed at the next level .. for us that means at the State level meetings that start after these local meetings complete.

> ### BOB BERENDZEN

That's the coolest thing I've ever heard.

CHRIS ZAMBERLAN
I thought you'd like that.

MATT WOODS
Okay, it seems everyone is done
voting.

MATT taps a few times on his tablet...

MATT WOODS
And here are the results. 47% say Not
concerned. 23% say A little
concerned. 10% say Concerned and 20%
say Very concerned.

MATT WOODS
Does anyone wish to champion the "Not
concerned" position to attempt to
persuade the 30%?

BOB BERENDZEN
(speaks without the floor, jumps up)
You bet I do.

DEAN SHILLITO
Hand please. Raise your hand to get
the floor.

BOB raises his hand while still standing.

BOB BERENDZEN
(embarrased)
Oh, okay.

MATT WOODS
Okay, Bob, let it rip. Convince us
that there is no concern that Tech

Branch will increase the size of
Federal government.

BOB BERENDZEN

As I mentioned before, I'm a Computer
Scientist. Technology, throughout
history, has made people more
efficient. Technology catapults
productivity. The Tech Branch will
bring modern levels of productivity
where it's most needed. Agencies with
departments that today need 100
people to process 10,000 whatever
each year will do the job with 50, or
20. Multiply that by 1000 and scale
it up to a population of millions of
citizens and I predict in less than
10 years Federal government will no
longer be the number one employer in
the USA.

KEITH raises his hand

KEITH

May I, Matt?

MATT WOODS

Yes, Keith. Jump in.

KEITH

Bob, *history* has proven that
government never shrinks. What makes
you think it will? Just because of
the Tech Branch?

BOB BERENDZEN

Government has never been able to
shrink for one simple reason. It has

never been anyone's *job* to shrink it!
Sure, a few citizen whine and moan
that government should be small and
unobtrusive, yada, yada, spend less
money and have no debt. Where has
that gotten us? Nowhere.

Crowd taps pens and pencils to show agreement.

> ### BOB BERENDZEN
> WHAT has that gotten us.. bigger
> government out of every
> administration in my lifetime, no
> matter the party.

Pens and pencils tap louder

> ### BOB BERENDZEN
> Tech Branch changes that.

> ### KEITH
> But the Tech branch members are
> appointed by elected officials, which
> means politicians, which means
> politics and beholden to their
> sponsor.

CHRIS raises his hand

> ### CHRIS ZAMBERLAN
> Point of Order.

> ### DEAN SHILLITO
> Yes, Chris?

CHRIS stands

CHRIS ZAMBERLAN
The allegiance of Tech Branch members
is a different issue than the current
debate.

DEAN SHILLITO
Agreed, but it supersedes because it
challenges the credibility of the
Tech branch at all. I suggest we go
to the app with a new open vote to
address this issue before going back
to Size of government. All in favor?

Many in the crowd yell out "aye"

DEAN SHILLITO
All opposed?

Just a few "nay"

DEAN SHILLITO
Ayes have it. I'll enter the open
vote now.

BOB BERENDZEN
(to Chris, not sure what to think)
This is interesting.

CHRIS ZAMBERLAN
(to Bob)
It is.. but we're forgetting
something.

CHRIS ZAMBERLAN
(to all)
Point of order, Dean.

DEAN SHILLITO

Yes, Chris?

CHRIS ZAMBERLAN

Since Keith raised a point in an attempt to defeat Bob's position in the debate, Bob gets to make his best case against Keith's point to convince the members *before* the vote.

DEAN SHILLITO

Good point. Go for it Bob, while I'm creating the open vote.

BOB BERENDZEN
(surprised)

Umm... Okay, Keith asserts that because Tech branch members are appointed to their positions by elected officials they will do the bidding of their sponsors because their allegiance will always be to them. Yes?

MATT shakes his head in disbelief pleased at how quickly and how well Bob fits into the group.

KEITH

Yes.

BOB BERENDZEN

I disagree for at least 2 reasons. First of all, the so-called sponsor has no power of recall after the appointment is made. The sponsor doesn't control the member's pay or job performance appraisal or anything remotely resembling a boss-employee relationship. But the best reason to believe in allegiance to the sponsor won't taint the integrity of the Tech branch is simply this: The people who are qualified to become members. Scientists, Engineers, Professors, Thinkers, Doctors, Researchers, specialists in many fields gathering from perhaps around the globe, coming together to participate in debate and analysis and policy contributions in a way that the world has never seen before quite like this.

BOB BERENDZEN

These people's allegiance will be to truth. They know that when they stand to make an argument or submit a proposal or an analysis of a policy that their reputation is on the line. A reputation they've worked their entire adult life to craft. It will not easily be discarded making false arguments the way politicians do. I know, I am one. I'm qualified to be a charter member.

BOB pauses for effect.

BOB BERENDZEN

Everyone expects politicians to be political and to spin instead of tell the truth. There are no consequences for believing one thing, saying another and doing a third if you're a politician.

BOB BERENDZEN

No one who would hire Tech branch
members after their term is up will
be quite so forgiving for the simple
fact that no one can afford to
possibly be spun by them when the
future of a billion dollar company
lays in the balance on a decision
about this or that fabrication method
for a new generation of silicon chip,
for example. That's gotta be the
primary reason the Amendment calls
for everything Tech branch does to be
public record.

KEITH

Sold me.

MATT WOODS

Let's vote, since it's loaded up.

CHRIS ZAMBERLAN
(whispers to Bob)

Very good job.

A few minutes go by. People mumbling to each other about the
thunderous defense of a position they just heard.

MATT WOODS

And the votes are in... 97% say Tech
branch members allegiance will be to
truth, not their sponsor. Boy, it's
rare to see that kind of unanimity.
Well argued.

MATT refocuses back to the first debate.

> ### MATT WOODS
> So, since the integrity of Tech branch is accepted, perhaps it's best we re-vote on the size of govt issue to see where we stand.

> ### DEAN SHILLITO
> Anyone opposed?

silence from the audience

> ### DEAN SHILLITO
> Let's vote.

> ### BOB BERENDZEN
> (to Chris)
> How do we know when the issue is closed?

> ### CHRIS ZAMBERLAN
> You'll see.

A brief minute goes by. MATT glances at his tablet.

> ### MATT WOODS
> That was fast. Everyone is in. 100% now say "Not concerned." WOW

Loud pen and pencil tapping.

> ### MATT WOODS
> Well done everyone. Excellent exchange. This is what CCC is about. Moving on to the last question of the night.

> ### MATT WOODS
> Section 8. Does the Citizen Voting System handle only votes controlled

by Federal government or by State
elected officials too?

MATT WOODS
Good question. The last sentence
could've brought in State governments
into the mix, but it didn't.

MATT WOODS
Any thoughts on the answer?

MARK COUGHLIN raises his hand

MATT WOODS
Yes, Mark?

MARK stands

MARK COUGHLIN
This was my question. Frankly I don't
know what I think. I don't know if I
want vote questions coming from the
States as well as Federal government
or not. I can see arguments for both
sides. That's why I asked the
question.

MATT WOODS
Okay. Perhaps we can get someone to
jump into the debate in favor of vote
questions coming from State
government too.

silence

MATT WOODS
(does his Ben Stein impersonation)
Anyone?

silence

                    MATT WOODS
   Anyone?

BOB raises his hand this time.

                    MATT WOODS
   Yes, Bob. You're on a roll. Help us
   out.

                    BOB BERENDZEN
   Perhaps State government is
   purposefully not mentioned, by
   design, so that after the system is a
   success, State governments will be
   willing to *pay* to participate.

                    MATT WOODS
   hmmm. Pay?

                    BOB BERENDZEN
   Sure a system for voting like this
   wouldn't be a huge expense, but it
   wouldn't be free. Why not have Tech
   branch do the heavy lifting to build
   the right system and build the system
   right, then, offer use of it to the
   States, for a price. A price that
   covers operations cost, plus a
   little. You said yourself, Dan's a
   capitalist.

                    MATT WOODS
   True. I could see each week a
   question that originates from Federal
   government and one from State
   government.

LAURA raises her hand

                    MATT WOODS
     Yes, Laura. Jump in.

LAURA stands.

                       LAURA
     If you and Bob are both right it
     would lead to a situation where even
     more people are motivated to vote,
     which is clearly an objective spelled
     out in the rationale.

                    MATT WOODS
     How so? Why would more people vote?
     Just because there are more
     questions?

                       LAURA
     No, it's not the number of question,
     per se, it's the origin, the source.
     The topics, actually. Some people get
     excited about local issues, some
     about national. In any given week, as
     long as there is one question
     relevant to an individual citizen,
     that citizen is likely to show up and
     vote on them all.

                   BOB BERENDZEN
     I totally understand that logic, but
     why not spell that out?

CHRIS raises his hand.

                    MATT WOODS
     Yes. Chris. Stand. What do you think?

CHRIS ZAMBERLAN

Perhaps *we're* meant change section 8
to include the States.

AHA moment shared by the crowd. Pens & pencils tapping.

MATT WOODS

Could be. Could be. What do you
think? Do you and Bob want to take an
action item to work on a re-write and
submit it before the next meeting?

BOB BERENDZEN

Not me.

MATT WOODS

Are you sure?

BOB BERENDZEN

Thanks, but to be honest with you...
I have an idea for Section *nine*.
Something is missing from the
Amendment that Tech Branch must do.

MATT WOODS
(impressed)

So soon? Really? Do tell.

CHRIS ZAMBERLAN
(interrupting)

No, no. Not now. Let him work on it
for a future meeting. I'm 99% sure I
know what it is, because we've talked
about his idea before. It's terrific.
It's why I brought him into the group
actually. As we've all seen tonight,
Bob is... and I don't say this
lightly... Dan-Farfan-kind-of-smart.

Crowd taps pens and pencils to show agreement.

MATT WOODS
Okay. Fantastic. We'll give Bob an action item for new Section 9 and Chris, you get one for Section 8 re-write? Yes?

CHRIS ZAMBERLAN
Yes. Anyone who wants to help can message me in the CCC app. Laura and Mark, I want you two to at least review my draft, okay?

LAURA
No problem.

MARK COUGHLIN
My pleasure.

MATT WOODS
John, give us a recap.

JOHN VODA
Action item 8 goes to Bob Berendzen (don't forget to install the mobile app) to propose Section 9 for Tech Branch. Due before next meeting. Okay, Bob?

BOB BERENDZEN
(a little stunned)

Okay.

DEAN SHILLITO
Thanks. Action Item 9 goes to Chris Zamberlan. Rewrite Section 8 Tech

Branch to include State involvement.
Okay, Chris?

CHRIS ZAMBERLAN
Yes. And Laura & Mark agreed to
review.

JOHN VODA
Good point. Okay. Got it. Okay,
Laura?

LAURA
All good.

JOHN VODA
Okay, Mark?

MARK COUGHLIN
Wouldn't miss it.

MATT WOODS
Okay. That was the last question on
the last Section. You know what that
means... John, recap the minutes.

JOHN reads the Action Items, agreements and open questions
recorded throughout the evening. Read back to back it's an
impressive collection of serious items.

BOB BERENDZEN
(to CHRIS)
Impressive.

CHRIS ZAMBERLAN
(to Bob)
Yes. It certainly is. And you were
great. New people almost never

participate. And to earn an Action
Item of your own... that's *huge*.

MATT WOODS

Okay everyone. Great night. Thank you
so much. Really good contributions
and discussions. I'm excited to see
what ya'll do with these Action Items
for next meeting. Round of Applause!

Applause

MATT WOODS

Good night. Drive safely, because
I'll be walking!

With that the meeting ends.

BOB BERENDZEN

I'll be honest with you. I wasn't
planning to participate at all. It
was just so... so... something

CHRIS ZAMBERLAN

I know. And I know what your Section
9 is. Scorecard, right?

BOB BERENDZEN
(smiling)
Yes. Role of Govt Scorecard.

CHRIS ZAMBERLAN

It's a perfect assignment for Tech
Branch.

BOB BERENDZEN

Think people will like it?

CHRIS ZAMBERLAN
You kidding? They'll love it...
unless you completely blow it and
make it suck.

BOB BERENDZEN
(jokingly)
Well, there is always that.

CHRIS ZAMBERLAN
Let's go catch up with Laura and
Keith.

BOB BERENDZEN
(excited)
No, I gotta get home, get the app,
find my writeup on Scorecard, and
then..

CHRIS ZAMBERLAN
Okay. Okay. I get it. I've created a
monster. Don't forget you still have
to work tomorrow.

BOB BERENDZEN
(laughing)
Yes. Good. Thanks. Work. Paycheck.
These are things that don't suck.

CHRIS stands and extends his hand.

CHRIS ZAMBERLAN
See you tomorrow. I'm going to catch
up with some folks and see if anyone
has thoughts about my Action Item.
Some don't like to speak up during
the meeting.

BOB stand and shakes his hand.

                    BOB BERENDZEN
        Good night. And thanks again. You're
        a good friend

                    CHRIS ZAMBERLAN
        My pleasure.

FADE OUT:

Citizen Constitutional Convention™ - Act III
Copyright 2013 Dan Farfan

FADE IN:

INT. NIGHT. BOB'S HOME OFFICE

BOB rifles through a draw of hand written paper notes about projects large and small from times long since passed and not so long ago. He's looking for the brainstorm regarding "Role of Govt Scorecard."

> BOB BERENDZEN
> (to himself)
> I know it's here... somewhere. Books?
> No. TV shows? No. Screenplays? No.
> Websites! Yes, good.

BOB's looking through the correct folder now

> BOB BERENDZEN
> (to himself)
> Okay. No, no, no. Oh, boy that's
> still a good idea, but not the right
> one. No, no.... yes! Role of Govt
> Scorecard. Bingo!

Having found the paperwork he sought, BOB sits at the computer

> BOB BERENDZEN
> (to himself)
> Now, the spreadsheet and
> powerpoint...

Clicking and scrolling and looking and..

BOB BERENDZEN
(to himself)

BINGO again!

BOB BERENDZEN
(reading from screen)

"Role of Govt Scorecard." Six
players. Twenty seven sectors. 154
responsibilities.

BOB BERENDZEN
(to himself)

Wow this is big. I hope not too big.

As BOB reads over the material from his handwritten notes and computer files he searches for the key words and phrases that capture the essence of the idea. THAT is what he needs to craft a section 9 for the Tech Branch Amendment. Comfortable that he's put the whole concept back into the front of his mind BOB wonders.

BOB BERENDZEN
(to himself)

What the heck am I doing? Really. I'm
writing an Amendment to the
Constitution?! THE U.S. Constitution.
Crazy. Well, not a whole Amendment.
Just a new section

With that he hears Matt's words from earlier...

MATT WOODS
(flashback audio)

""Never doubt that a small group of
thoughtful, committed citizens can
change the world; indeed, it's the
only thing that ever has."

BOB BERENDZEN
(to himself)

Yes, thoughtful and committed. I can fake those.

BOB chuckles

BOB BERENDZEN
(to himself)

Here goes... "Section 9. The Technology branch shall specify, design and oversee internal or external creation of and use of by citizens of the United States of America...

FADE TO

INT HIGH SCHOOL GYM

BOB standing presenting his proposed section

"..a website named RoleOf.gov whose purpose is to crowdsource the definition and specification of what each of the six participant groups (Citizens, For-profit companies, Non-profit companies, Local, State and Federal government) should be responsible for vis a vis the operation of the country."

Dead silence in the room, because no one has any idea what that really means.

BOB BERENDZEN

And on the next slide.. is the rationale. "Section 9 - Rationale. For decades the so-called debate about the proper role of government has produced no benefits, changed no minds and clarified no issues. Government does more and more every year with virtually no restraint. Further, every debate about any particular topic usually degenerates into a battle of emotional anecdotes rather than reasoned solution.

RoleOf.gov removes all the abstractness from the conceptual arguments about who should do what. RoleOf.gov contains an interactive scorecard where politicians and citizens alike can visit, vote their opinion, read scholarly works and even compare their dream scorecard against the famous systems of the past such as Stalin's Soviet Union or Hitler's Germany. Won't you be surprised when you realize how much your view of a "more perfect union" best matches Mao's!!

List the six players across the top of the page, list the 27 sectors of the economy such as Education, Energy, Charity, Transportation... down the left side. Then in each sector is a number "responsibilities" - 154 in all. The intersection of a Player and a responsibility in a sector is a cell. In each cell contains a "Y" for yes or an "N" for no. Yes or no, over and over. Who should do what. Should Federal govt be a charity? Yes or No.

Pens and Pencils tapping

BOB BERENDZEN
Do you want Federal government to *be* a charity or should only Non-profit companies be charities? Visit RoleOf.gov and make your voice heard.

If our elected officials seek most to know where we are going so that they may scramble to the front to lead us there, RoleOf.gov is the clearest picture possible shining the brightest light possible showing the way.

Pens and pencils tapping wildly.

BOB BERENDZEN
And on the next few slides is the list of all the sectors and the responsibilities inside each. Those of you with the CCC mobile app can access the full list for your careful review. Please propose changes or additions as you think of them.

BOB looks to MATT

BOB BERENDZEN
That's all I have.

MATT WOODS
Let's here it everyone. Well done, Bob

Applause.

MATT WOODS
Okay, let's open the floor to feedback. Hands first please.

KEITH

I love it. I see it. I want to visit
the website right away. But the
rationale seems very wordy.

Pens and pencils tapping.

KEITH

The phrase about scrambling to the
front to lead us is a fine debate
point supporting the notion, but it's
not appropriate for the text of
Constitution itself.

Pens and pencils tapping.

KEITH

I submitted some wording changes via
the CCC mobile app for consideration.

KEITH points to the big screen

MATT WOODS

Yes. I see your feedback here. One
second I can put them on the screen.

Up on the screen, one by one each paragraph "before" and
"proposed." Each one is an improvement in text, tone and style
that impresses even BOB.

BOB BERENDZEN

I have to say, I'm impressed with the
rewrite. Very well done. Thank you
very much, Keith

KEITH

No need to thank me. It's your
brilliant idea.

LAURA raises her hand

MATT WOODS

Yes, Laura.

LAURA

I don't really mind that the
rationale is long. Longest of all in
the entire book, I think. I don't
mind that. In fact I think there
might be a missing paragraph from the
rationale.

MATT WOODS

Do tell.

LAURA

Since Tech Branch is such a new and
for the most part a completely
unexpected creation, it'll be a
challenge to first introduce it, then
educate the population, then build
trust, and so on and so on.
RoleOf.gov is a terrific ice breaker
so to speak. From a website open to
all citizens comes something
interactive to do, something to learn
about, something to share with others
who agree and even those who don't..
from all of that comes the
introduction to the Tech Branch and
all it does and will do, how, when,
why, etc.

Pens and pencils tapping

LAURA

That makes RoleOf.gov very important
to the success of Tech Branch and
citizens bonding.

MATT WOODS

I believe that's a really good point.
Another way to look at it is that
it's never been anyone's job in
government to ask citizens what their
vision for who should do what to make
the operation of the country better,
stronger, faster or even just
smoother - until Tech Branch.

LAURA

Yes. Exactly. So, I'd like to take an
action item to write an additional
paragraph to the Section 9 Rationale
for the Tech Branch Amendment.

DEAN SHILLITO

Any objections?

Silence, including BOB

MATT WOODS

You are okay with the help, right
Bob? This is how we roll.

BOB BERENDZEN

Yes. Certainly. I look forward to
reading it, Laura.

LAURA

Great.

MATT WOODS
If there are no other questions,
issues or challenges regarding
Section 9, let's move on.

Everyone sits after Dean's hand gesture.

CHRIS ZAMBERLAN
(whispers to Bob)
You nailed it. First try. A few minor
revisions. One new paragraph. You
rocked it.

BOB BERENDZEN
(very proud, whispers to Chris)
Thanks. Thanks a lot.

MATT continues the meeting in the background

CHRIS ZAMBERLAN
(whispers to Bob)
Wouldn't surprise me if you become
the first person elected to go to the
Statewide CCC.

BOB BERENDZEN
(surprised)
What? Who, me?

CHRIS gives BOB a supportive reassuring look. A few moments
go by with the local CCC meeting continuing.

BOB BERENDZEN
(whispers to Chris)
How does *that* work?

FADE TO BLACK

ABOUT THE AUTHOR

Dan Farfan is a three time patent–granted veteran Computer Scientist with over 30 years experience in the automotive, telecommunications and homeland security industries. His expertise lies in information management, languages and system architecture.

Dan's hobbies including writing books, solving large problems, writing screenplays and ballroom dancing. His dream of winning the coveted mirrorball Dancing with the Stars trophy is unfulfilled, so far. :-)